AN ALBUM OF THE
SEVENTIES

BY DOROTHY AND THOMAS HOOBLER

Franklin Watts

New York | London | Toronto | Sydney

1981

Cover photographs courtesy of Movie Star News, National Archives/Nixon Presidential Materials Project, Casio, Romanian Library, New York City, and Wide World Photos.

Interior photographs courtesy of Wide World Photos: opp. p. 1 (top), pp. 8 (top and bottom), 11, 12 (left), 15 (top and bottom), 16, 20 (top), 31 (top right), 43 (bottom right), 48 (bottom right), 54 (top), 70, 78 (top), 82 (left and right), 83, 84, 85, 87; Department of Energy: opp. p. 1 (middle), pp. 24 (right), 27 (top right), 27 (bottom left/photo by Jack Schneider); U.S. Navy: opp. p. 1 (bottom), 35 (top left and top right); Valley Dispatch News: p. 3; U.S. Army: pp. 4 (all), 31 (top left); Viet-Nam Photo Service: p. 7; W. W. Norton Co./Steve Northrup: p. 12 (right); National Archives/Nixon Presidential Materials Project: pp. 19 (top and bottom), 20 (bottom); Thomas Hoobler: pp. 23, 28 (bottom), 39 (top left and top right); Religious News Service: pp. 24 (left), 31 (bottom), 36 (all; middle photo by Don Rutledge, bottom left photo by John Lei); Alyeska Pipeline Service Company: p. 27 (top left); Westinghouse: p. 27 (bottom right, photo by Jack Merhaut); United Nations: pp. 28 (top), 43 (left, photo by J. K. Isaac, and top right), 48 (top, CIDA/WHITE); Stanley Forman/Boston Herald American: p. 32; National Archives: p. 35 (bottom); Sasson Jeans, Inc.: p. 39 (bottom); Casio: p. 40 (top and bottom left); McDonald's Corporation: p. 40 (upper left); Sony Corp.: p. 40 (upper right); Motorola: p. 40 (middle left); Coleco: p. 40 (lower right); NASA: pp. 44 (top and bottom), 51 (left and right), 52 (top and bottom), 53; Consulate General of Israel, New York: p. 47 (top and bottom); NACLA/MAGNUM/Susan Meiselas: p. 48 (bottom left); Bell Labs: p. 54 (bottom); Universal Pictures: p. 57; Movie Star News: pp. 58 (all), 59 (left and right), 60, 63 (top and bottom), 64, 81, 86 (bottom); PBS: p. 66 (top and bottom); Casablanca Record and Film Works: p. 67 (top); MCA: p. 67 (bottom); Farrar Straus Giroux/Jerry Bauer: p. 69 (top); Beverly Sills: p. 69 (bottom left); WNET/13: p. 69 (bottom right); Women's Tennis Association/Cheryl A. Traendly: pp. 72 (left), 79 (left); Goodyear Tire & Rubber Co.: p. 72 (right); Atlanta Braves: p. 73; Don King Productions, Inc.: p. 75; Buffalo Bills: p. 76 (left); Dallas Cowboys: p. 76 (right); New York Cosmos: p. 78 (bottom left); Romanian Library, New York City: p. 78 (bottom right); Los Angeles Lakers: p. 79 (right); American Broadcasting Company: p. 86 (top).

Library of Congress Cataloging in Publication Data

Hoobler, Dorothy.
An album of the seventies.

Includes index.
Summary: Highlights the notable events
and personalities of the 1970s.
1. History, Modern—1945–
—Juvenile literature.
[1. History, Modern—1945–   ]
I. Hoobler, Thomas. II. Title.
D848.H66   909.82'7   81-3347
ISBN 0-531-04322-3   AACR2

CONTENTS

AN ALBUM OF THE
SEVENTIES

Left: Iranian students demonstrating in front of the American Embassy in Teheran, where American hostages were being held.

Above: a billboard message urging gasoline conservation. The sign sums up a major fear of the 1970s, that the world's resources were running out. Right: a young spectator at a Bicentennial celebration wears his feelings on his T-shirt. T-shirt messages, not always so optimistic, were an omnipresent feature of the 1970s.

A SENSE OF LIMITS

The seizure of the American Embassy in Teheran, Iran, by militant students in November 1979 brought to a crashing end a decade that had shocked and shaken Americans. In the 1970s, for the first time since World War II, the United States realized that it was no longer uncontestedly number one in world affairs.

The oil-producing nations used their control of the world's oil supplies to send the price of gasoline at the pump skyrocketing. The spiraling price of energy fueled raging inflation that sometimes reached levels near 20 percent. At the same time, lagging American productivity and efficiency weakened the country's economy in worldwide competition with western Europe and Japan. For Americans, the problems they faced were new in their history, bringing a sense of the limits of growth and opportunity.

America faced these problems in a decade when distrust and discontent with government was at an all-time high. The war in Vietnam ended in ignominious defeat. Watergate and other scandals involving corporate and government officials eroded respect for the traditional ruling institutions.

The biggest social change of the decade was the women's movement, which revolutionized American society. Women won the right to opportunities that had not been open to them before. These opportunities and rising inflation led to the rapid growth of two-income families in which both husband and wife shared the burdens of house and workplace.

For some, the seventies was the "me decade," in which great numbers of people sought individual fulfillment in religious cults, self-awareness groups, and the general desire to "get my head together." The concerns with self brought about an attitude of selfishness, as Americans competed with each other to acquire a share of what seemed to be an ever-shrinking pie.

Yet Americans had weathered difficulties before, and there remained hopeful signs.

(1)

COMING HOME

Vietnamization

When Richard Nixon became president in 1969, the majority of Americans were tired of the war in Vietnam. Protests over the war were opening serious rifts in American society. Nixon announced his policy of Vietnamization—letting the Asian allies fight their own war with military and technical help from the United States. That year Nixon announced the first of his troop withdrawals from Vietnam. But secretly, Nixon was expanding the war. In 1969, unknown to all but a few top military people and Nixon advisers, the United States began bombing Cambodian territory adjacent to Vietnam.

In 1970 a coup in Cambodia brought right-wing Lon Nol to power in place of Prince Norodom Sihanouk. On April 30, Nixon announced that the United States and South Vietnam were attacking bases in Cambodia which were arms depots and staging areas for North Vietnamese troops. The first official extension of the war into Cambodia brought criticism and protest in the United States.

Among the college campuses where protests occurred was Kent State in Ohio, where students burned down the ROTC building. Ohio Governor James Rhodes called in the National Guard. On May 4, National Guard forces opened fire on student demonstrators; four were killed and eleven wounded. The killings "brought the war home," shocked the nation, and brought on the first American general student strike, in which about four hundred colleges were closed. On May 9, over one hundred thousand students marched on Washington as a protest against Kent State and the Vietnam War.

The Pentagon Papers

On June 13, 1971, readers of *The New York Times* were startled by the first installment of what were to be called the Pentagon Papers. These documents were a secret Defense Department history of

**A Kent State University student reacts
with horror to the sight of a student
shot by National Guardsmen on May 4, 1970.**

United States decision making on Southeast Asia from the 1950s to 1968. They were leaked to the *Times* by former Defense Department analyst Daniel Ellsberg, a former hawk who had joined the growing movement against the war.

Publication of the report caused considerable anger in the White House. The Justice Department obtained an injunction to force the *Times* to stop publishing the serialized report after three days. But the *Washington Post* obtained its own copy of the Pentagon Papers and resumed the publication. The Supreme Court finally ruled that publication of the documents was constitutional and protected.

Ellsberg, however, was indicted for theft of government documents. The White House formed a group of investigators called the Plumbers (to stop leaks) to find incriminating information about Ellsberg. G. Gordon Liddy and E. Howard Hunt, two Plumbers who would later become famous for their other activities in the Watergate scandals, broke into the office of Ellsberg's psychiatrist. When the break-in was revealed in 1973, Judge William Matthew Byrne, presiding at Ellsberg's trial, dismissed the case.

Defeat

Throughout Nixon's first term in office, the war dragged on. Even with Vietnamization, the United States remained heavily involved through massive air support. South Vietnamese troops further displayed their inability to carry on the war alone with an unsuccessful attempt

Top left: an American infantry company crosses a stream in South Vietnam while on a "search and clear" operation. Top right: American troops roll into a Cambodian village, finding buildings and shops in ruin—but no sign of the North Vietnamese enemy. Lower left: an American howitzer crew in action four miles south of the DMZ (Demilitarized Zone), which divided North and South Vietnam. Lower right: South Vietnamese soldiers in Laos moving through thick tropical vegetation.

to root out North Vietnamese bases in Laos in 1971. Though Nixon denied the mission was a failure, television showed South Vietnamese soldiers running from combat and trying desperately to get away in American helicopters.

On March 30, 1972, North Vietnamese soldiers streamed across the demilitarized zone that divided Vietnam in the biggest offensive since Tet in 1968. The offensive put tremendous pressure on the Nixon Administration to step up negotiations for peace. National Security Adviser Henry Kissinger and North Vietnamese representative Le Duc Tho met regularly to discuss the terms of American withdrawal. Just before the 1972 elections, Kissinger announced that the negotiations had been fruitful and, "Peace is at hand."

After Nixon's election victory, however, peace remained elusive. The South Vietnamese leader, Nguyen Van Thieu, refused to go along with Kissinger's concessions. To force the North Vietnamese to better terms and "peace with honor," the United States, at the end of December 1972, unleashed the most vicious bombing of the war. Intense bombing of Hanoi and Haiphong continued for days in what became known as "the Christmas bombing," an act Nixon would later say was "the most difficult decision I've made as president." The news of the destruction of hospitals and civilian centers brought renewed protests and revulsion against America's position in the war.

Refugees in Ben Cat, Binh Duong Province in South Vietnam, an area north of Saigon, line up to receive a share of the rice that was seized by the South Vietnamese in a raid on the Vietcong. During this raid, 2,384 tons of rice were captured, along with 12,405 hand grenades, 128 individual weapons, 752 torpedoes, and several truckloads of other military supplies.

Above: this Pulitzer Prize-winning photograph shows the family of a returning prisoner of war running to greet him in March 1973. Left: American National Security Adviser Henry A. Kissinger (right) and Le Duc Tho, North Vietnam's chief negotiator, met near Paris in May 1973 to discuss ways to implement the peace agreement.

On January 23, 1973, Kissinger and Le Duc Tho initialled a peace agreement in Paris, for which they were later jointly awarded the Nobel Peace Prize. The accord called for a ceasefire and the withdrawal of American troops from all of Vietnam. North Vietnamese troops were permitted to remain where they were. In return there was to be a prompt return of American prisoners of war. There was, however, no agreement on Cambodia. On March 29, the last American soldiers left Vietnam.

After Congress halted the bombing of Cambodia in August 1973, American involvement in Vietnam was limited to the shipment of supplies. The war went on, now widened to include Cambodia and Laos as well as Vietnam, as Communist forces continued the fight, seeking to control all of the Indo-Chinese peninsula.

In early 1975 the North Vietnamese began a new offensive into South Vietnam. With the South Vietnamese troops badly led and generally unable to resist, the end came with shocking swiftness, as Americans watched on their televisions. On March 30, Danang fell, and remnants of the South Vietnamese forces along with civilians streamed southward toward Saigon. In Cambodia, the Lon Nol government was besieged, controlling only the environs of its capital, Phnom Phenh.

By the end of April the North Vietnamese massed to attack Saigon. The last four hundred American civilians were shuttled in helicopters from the embassy roof to the safety of a Navy ship on the morning of April 30. The United States announced the end of the struggle and the first major military defeat in its history. Ignominiously, the United States had not been able to rescue many of the pro-American Vietnamese, leaving them to an uncertain future.

In human terms, the cost of the Vietnam War to the United States was fifty-seven thousand dead and many more wounded and maimed for life. The social and international cost to the country was more widespread. Many more Asians had died in the futile effort. Laos and Cambodia soon fell, and the repressive government that replaced Lon Nol instituted one of the bloodiest regimes in human history, threatening finally the existence of the Cambodian people.

The effects in the United States included tremendous civil discontent, a lingering distrust of government due to a pattern of government deception, and the beginnings of the inflation which devastated America throughout the 1970s.

(9)

SCANDAL

A "Third-Rate Burglary"

In the early morning hours of June 17, 1972, police apprehended five burglars in the Democratic party headquarters in the Watergate hotel–apartment complex in Washington, D.C. The five men were well dressed and had sophisticated electronic listening devices. In their pockets police found about twelve hundred dollars, mostly in one-hundred-dollar bills. From this petty crime spread a scandal that would bring down the President of the United States and cast doubt on the integrity of the American political system.

It was soon discovered that one of the burglars, James McCord, was a security employee at President Nixon's Committee to Re-Elect the President (dubbed CREEP). A notebook belonging to one of the burglars mentioned the name and White House phone number of E. Howard Hunt. On September 15, indictments were handed down against the five burglars, Hunt, and G. Gordon Liddy, who was a lawyer at CREEP at the time of the burglary.

The news media at first gave little attention to the case. But two little-known reporters from the *Washington Post,* Bob Woodward and Carl Bernstein, published a continuing series of stories on the case. In October they published news of a secret fund controlled by former Attorney General John Mitchell and White House Chief of Staff H. R. (Bob) Haldeman. They also uncovered a series of campaign dirty tricks perpetrated by Nixon campaign workers.

Ironically, dirty tricks and break-ins had been quite unnecessary to secure a Nixon victory in the election of 1972. The Democratic nomination had been captured by a leading liberal opponent of the Vietnam War, South Dakota's Senator George McGovern. Alabama's Governor George Wallace had also sought the nomination, but had been shot and paralyzed at a Laurel, Maryland, shopping center in May.

**The Watergate hotel–apartment complex
became the symbol of a series of scandals
that finally destroyed the Nixon presidency.**

Left: Democratic presidential nominee Senator George
McGovern with his first vice-presidential candidate, Senator
Thomas Eagleton. Right: Judge John J. Sirica was instrumental
in breaking the coverup in the Watergate case by closely
questioning witnesses and threatening long prison terms.

McGovern chose as his running mate Missouri Senator Thomas Eagleton. Immediately after the convention, the story broke that Eagleton had once been treated for psychological problems. At first McGovern claimed to be behind Eagleton "one thousand percent," but shortly afterward asked him to leave the ticket.

The vice-presidential flap and McGovern's liberal politics ruined his chances for the presidency. McGovern lost the election by the most lopsided plurality in history, carrying only Massachusetts and the District of Columbia. The 1972 elections were the first in which the 26th amendment was in force, allowing 18-year-olds to vote.

The Cover-Up Unfolds

In January 1973 the trial of the seven Watergate defendants started in the courtroom of Judge John Sirica. Five pleaded guilty and the two others, Liddy and McCord, were found guilty by a jury on January 30. Sirica, who was known for his toughness on the bench, was not satisfied that the truth in the case had been reached. Stories circulated that the defendants had been paid to remain silent. Sirica threatened harsh sentences for the men. On February 7, the Senate voted to establish a select committee to investigate the burglary and other reported campaign irregularities.

At the sentencing of McCord and Liddy on March 23, Judge Sirica read a letter he had received from McCord. McCord charged that perjury had been committed at the trial and that higher-ups were involved in the burglary. The letter caused a sensation. Others who had been involved now rushed to plead with the prosecutors for special treatment; they also leaked self-justifying stories to the press.

New stories appeared daily about the Executive branch's misdeeds and misuse of agencies such as the CIA and FBI. On April 17, Nixon spoke of "major developments" in the Watergate case. Two days later White House Counsel John Dean announced ominously that he would not be made a scapegoat in the Watergate affair. At the end of April the news broke about Hunt and Liddy's earlier involvement in the Ellsberg case. Demands were voiced for a special prosecutor, and Archibald Cox was to investigate the widening scandal.

On April 30, Nixon gave a televised speech in which he announced the resignations of Haldeman, John Ehrlichman, his chief domestic adviser, and Attorney General Richard Kleindienst. Nixon also fired John Dean from the White House staff. Although he admitted mistakes in not acting sooner to bring out all the facts in the case, Nixon denied any substantial involvement in the affair.

In the middle of May 1973 the nation watched as the Senate Select Committee opened its televised hearings. Chaired by Democratic Senator Sam Ervin, the hearings unfolded like a complicated and fascinating soap opera.

McCord and CREEP Deputy Director Jeb Magruder described the inception of a program to illegally sabotage the Democratic campaign—beginning in the office of John Mitchell, then Attorney General of the United States. The committee heard testimony describing early efforts at both the White House and CREEP to cover up the Watergate burglary with hush money and threats.

The highlight of the hearings was John Dean's five-day testimony beginning on June 25. He read page after page of a prepared statement in a droning, monotonous voice, detailing the atmosphere of hatred and distrust in the White House. Dean related how delighted the president had been the previous September when the indictments in the Watergate case had been limited to the seven defendants. The most damning single piece of testimony offered by Dean was his description of a conversation with the president on March 21 in which they had discussed hush money and other matters. Supposedly, Nixon had approved of the payment of money to Hunt to keep his mouth closed about the break-in.

Above: the members of the Senate Select Committee investigating Watergate became celebrities through television coverage of the hearings. Left to right: Vice-Chairman Senator Howard Baker of Tennessee; Senator Sam Ervin of North Carolina, the committee chairman; and Samuel Dash, counsel for the majority Democrats. Below: the star witness before the Senate Watergate committee was former White House counsel, John W. Dean III.

Resigned presidential aides H. R. Haldeman (center)
and John D. Ehrlichman (right) arrive at the Senate
office building during the Watergate hearings.

The White House vehemently denied Dean's story, but the wealth of detail he had provided and his apparent composure under cross-examination had shaken the public's confidence in the president.

When Nixon's former Chief of Staff, H. R. Haldeman, testified, he backed up Nixon's denial of Dean's account of the March 21 conversation. It seemed to be a case of Dean's word against Nixon's and Haldeman's. But on July 16 came an unexpected revelation: presidential aide Alexander Butterfield disclosed the existence of hidden tape recorders in the Oval Office and other places, that were voice-activated during all conversations. The Senate panel requested the tape of the key March 21 meeting, as well as other conversations. The White House refused.

Finally, Special Prosecutor Archibald Cox sued in court to get the tapes. Judge Sirica ruled on August 29 that the tapes should be turned over to him and he would delete items relating to national security and those parts that were irrelevant to the case. The White House appealed the decision.

A second major scandal now drew the nation's interest. Rumors spread through Washington that Vice-President Spiro Agnew had taken bribes from Maryland business interests. After protesting his innocence, Agnew suddenly resigned on October 10, pleading no contest to the charges in a court in Baltimore. In the first use of the twenty-fifth amendment covering presidential and vice-presidential succession, Nixon named House Republican Leader Gerald Ford as vice-president, and the Senate later voted confirmation.

On October 12, the Federal Court of Appeals upheld Judge Sirica's order that Nixon turn over the tapes. Rather than appeal the case to the Supreme Court, however, Nixon announced a "compromise": Nixon would turn over written summaries of the tapes' contents. Senator John Stennis would listen to the tapes to vouch for the accuracy of the summaries. In return Cox would agree to make no more demands on the White House. On October 20, Cox publicly refused the compromise and Nixon ordered Attorney General Elliott Richardson to fire him. Richardson resigned, and his deputy William Ruckelshaus refused to carry out the order. Finally Robert Bork officially fired Cox. The resignations and firing became known as the Saturday Night Massacre; an immense volume of protesting telegrams and letters poured into the White House.

Public reaction forced Nixon to agree to the appointment of another special prosecutor, Texas lawyer Leon Jaworski. Nixon had earlier agreed to turn over the requested tapes, although two of them were discovered missing from the storage area. Then it was announced that a crucial tape had an eighteen-minute gap in a conversation between the president and Haldeman. How the eighteen-minute erasure was made became an additional subject for investigation and public speculation.

On March 1, 1974, the Watergate Special Prosecution Force obtained grand jury indictments against seven high White House officials, including Mitchell, Haldeman, and Ehrlichman, for conspiracy to obstruct justice and other crimes. One clue to what the trial was likely to bring out was the indictment of Haldeman for perjury on his testimony about the March 21 conversation with Dean and Nixon. In the indictments, Nixon was named as an "unindicted co-conspirator," a fact that was not publicly revealed at the time. Jaworski was later to say that he did not feel a sitting president could be indicted for a crime, because the Constitution provided another procedure.

The other procedure was impeachment, and on May 9, the House Judiciary Committee began hearings on possible grounds for the impeachment of the president. The House Committee had asked for copies of the White House tapes, and Nixon stalled. On May 15 and 20 the committee subpoenaed the tapes.

In an attempt to assuage public opinion, Nixon released printed transcripts of the tapes in June. Reading the actual words of the president and his advisers for the first time, the public was shocked.

Above: Nixon's personal secretary, Rose Mary Woods, showing how she claimed to have accidentally erased part of the Nixon-Haldeman tape of June 20, 1972. Because it seemed improbable that she would have remained in that position for several minutes, her story was ridiculed, and the explanation was known as the "Rose Mary stretch." Below: President Nixon preparing to announce via television his intention to publicly release transcripts of the tapes.

Right: as people gathered in front of the Supreme Court waiting for a decision on the Nixon tapes, demonstrators appeared wearing Nixon and Kissinger masks. Below: having submitted his resignation as president, Nixon turns for a last salute before heading home to California.

Sprinkled liberally throughout the transcripts was the phrase "expletive deleted," which became a national joke. In no portion of the transcripts did Nixon himself ever seem to be concerned about the ethics of what was happening; to many, the evidence seemed to indicate that he condoned the coverup.

During the summer of 1974 Watergate and impeachment obsessed the country. On July 24, the Supreme Court ruled 8–0 that Nixon must turn over the actual tapes to the special prosecutor; he said he would obey the order.

The Judiciary Committee's debate over the articles of impeachment was televised. Headed by Representative Peter Rodino from New Jersey, the committee strived to carry on proceedings in a way that the country could agree was fair. On July 27, the committee approved an article of impeachment on the charge of obstructing justice. Two more articles were later approved. The next steps would be a vote by the full House, and then a trial in the Senate. There were still some in Congress who supported the president, and the impeachment process threatened to be an interminable agony.

Then, on August 5, the White House released the transcript of a June 23, 1972, conversation between Nixon and Haldeman. The tape transcript showed without doubt that Nixon had tried to use the CIA to obstruct the Watergate investigation from the start. This revelation was the "smoking gun" that removed any doubts about Nixon's guilt. Leaders of his own party advised him that there was no longer any support for his presidency. In a speech on the evening of August 8, Nixon announced that he would resign the next day but refused to admit guilt or remorse.

The following day, Nixon flew to his home in California, becoming the first president to resign. His successor, Gerald Ford, the first non-elected president to take office while his predecessor was still alive, announced, "Our long national nightmare is over."

Now that Nixon was no longer president, speculation grew as to whether he would be indicted on criminal charges. On September 8, President Ford cut off that possibility by granting Nixon a full pardon. Ford's action was highly controversial and probably cost him the chance of being elected president in his own right in 1976. President Ford named Nelson Rockefeller, former governor of New York, as his vice-president. For the first time, the country had both a president and vice-president who had not been elected.

DOLLARS AND POWER

Money

Economic affairs were more important during the 1970s than at any time since the Depression forty years earlier. Inflation plagued all of the world's developed nations. Worse, the inflation was sometimes coupled with high unemployment and economic recession. The unusual combination of inflation and recession gave rise to a new word: stagflation.

In the United States, the rate of inflation at the beginning of the decade was less than 6 percent—and even that was thought unacceptable by economists, politicians, and consumers. By the end of the decade, the inflation rate had climbed to around 13 percent.

The roots of the inflation lay in the mid-sixties, when President Johnson, unwilling to make Americans pay for the Vietnam War through higher taxes or cutbacks in social programs, gave the country "guns and butter." Huge government deficits were paid by printing more money, and the value of a dollar declined. At the beginning of the seventies, President Nixon said that control of inflation was his highest priority. In August 1971 Nixon ordered a temporary freeze on wages, prices, and rents. In addition he officially devalued the dollar and eliminated gold backing for American currency.

In 1972 the Soviet Union purchased huge quantities of grain from the United States, driving up the cost of food in the United States to unprecedented levels. With the Nixon controls expiring, inflation soared. Then the Arab oil embargo of 1973–74 caused oil prices to quadruple, and inflation set off in a wild spiral with energy and food leading the way. There were jokes about food prices rising between the time a customer entered the store and reached the checkout counter. But the price rises were real. Gasoline more than tripled in the decade, the price of an automobile doubled, rents and the price of a house followed the trend. Fueling the fire was the increasingly widespread use of credit cards, by which people could create their own credit so they could afford to maintain their standard of living in the face of rising costs.

(22)

The Susan B. Anthony dollar, the first American coin
to bear the likeness of a real woman, was first
issued in 1979. In whatever form, the dollar bought
less at the end of the decade than at the beginning.

Left: the seventies saw the rise of OPEC to the
status of a powerful economic force. Here, the
United Arab Emirates oil minister waves an auto-
matic weapon and joins other OPEC ministers after
a 1979 meeting that raised oil prices. Right:
these gas rationing coupons were produced but
never issued because rationing was regarded as
too unpopular for the government to try to impose.

President Ford announced a program to Whip Inflation Now (WIN), but his WIN buttons did no good. Appeals to business and labor to impose voluntary controls on prices and wages were unsuccessful. Inflation ebbed a bit after the recession of 1974, but when Jimmy Carter took office in 1977, the unemployment rate of about 8 percent caused a revision of economic priorities. In trying to spur economic activity to reduce unemployment, the Carter Administration set off a new round of inflation.

In addition, American industrial productivity was decreasing. It became more difficult for American-made goods to compete on the world market; on the other hand, foreign-made products sold increasingly well in the United States. Many Americans bought Japanese automobiles, for instance, because they had a reputation for higher quality and better gas mileage. By the end of the decade, nearly one-fourth of all cars sold in the United States were Japanese makes; one of Detroit's "big three" auto makers, Chrysler, teetered on the verge of bankruptcy and had to be bailed out by the government.

The economic crisis hit cities as well as businesses. In 1975 New York City narrowly averted bankruptcy. Other cities, particularly in the northeast and midwest, also faced the problems of declining tax bases and increased costs of municipal services.

The rising inflation caused social changes. Many wives took full-time jobs; the two-job family became the norm. The increases in family income pushed people into higher tax brackets, just as government was asking for more money to keep pace with inflation. Beginning in 1978, when California voters approved Proposition 13 to set a ceiling on property taxes, taxpayer revolts became commonplace. Ten other states passed similar legislation, limiting taxes.

Energy

No problem caused greater concern than the rising cost of energy. Cheap energy had fueled industrial growth since the 1950s. There was little planning for the day when oil, a finite resource, would become scarce, or run out. The Arab oil embargo of 1973–74 was a rude jolt. Americans argued over whether the shortage was real or artificially produced. The long lines of cars waiting to buy gasoline were real, as was the political threat behind the embargo. The Arab oil-producing countries cut off their shipments of oil, supposedly until Israel vacated territories seized in the Six-Day War of 1967. Though the embargo petered out the following year without achieving its aims, it illustrated the economic dependence of the United States on the nations of OPEC (Organization of Petroleum Exporting Countries), which included some non-Arab states.

On November 7, 1973, President Nixon proposed Project Independence, which was to make the United States self-sufficient in energy by 1980. The program was intended to increase drilling for domestic oil supplies, carry out research into nuclear energy, and find other energy alternatives. Americans were urged to drive slower and cut back on their home use of oil.

Project Independence was a flop. By the end of 1974 the United States was more dependent on foreign oil than ever, and the dependence grew as the decade progressed, even with the building of the Alaskan oil pipeline to bring Alaskan oil to "the lower 48." Alternative forms of energy such as coal, solar, geothermal, biomass, nuclear, and shale oil turned out to be more expensive than anticipated. There were other drawbacks. Coal polluted the atmosphere and was hazardous to miners. Nuclear energy brought many imponderable risks, a fact that would be driven home by the Three Mile Island accident in 1979.

One of the first problems newly inaugurated President Carter addressed in 1977 was energy. In a televised speech, he called the energy problem "the moral equivalent of war." The creation of a Department of Energy in 1977 underscored the administration's concern. But Carter's attention wandered, and so did the country's. Though energy prices were still going up, there were no more shortages (or gasoline lines) until 1979. It took Congress two years to pass Carter's proposed energy program, and even then it was a watered-down version.

The plan called for huge expenditures for alternative fuel development and further nuclear research. It also proposed the establishment of a body to help energy-producing businesses skirt federal regulations regarding pollution and environmental safety. This caused great consternation among conservationists and environmentalists. Money for developing alternative energy sources would come from an excess profits tax on the oil companies. The Carter plan promised real relief from dependence on foreign oil only by the end of the 1980s.

Top left: the Arab oil embargo gave impetus to building the Alaskan pipeline. The zigzag configuration of the pipeline allows thermal expansion
of the steel pipe. Top right: these solar cells turn the sun's radiant
energy directly into electricity, driving a 10-horsepower pump that pumps
water out of a reservoir and through an irrigation system in Nebraska.
Lower left: one of the effects of the oil embargo was a search for alternative fuels. Gasohol, a mixture of 10 percent alcohol and 90 percent
unleaded gasoline, was one alternative. Lower right: nuclear power was
the most controversial alternative energy source. Here, a woman is
inspecting nuclear fuel rods containing uranium dioxide fuel pellets.

Top: a "women's solidarity" march in New York City. Bottom: with more women working, daycare for their children became a necessity. Here, a daycare center in New York City.

STRUGGLE, CELEBRATION, AND ME

The Women's Movement

The greatest social change of the decade was in the status of women. Beginning with demands for equal pay for equal work, the women's movement soon began to reexamine the roles women were encouraged, or forbidden, to play in all areas of society. Playing on the old slogan, "Women's place is in the home," T-shirts appeared with the slogan, "Women's place is in the House and Senate." Nor was it confined to politics.

In the beginning of the decade, consciousness-raising groups around the country brought together women who found that they shared a frustration at what they perceived as an inferior role to men in the workplace, the military, the schools, and even the home. Demonstrations, pressure on local and national politicians, and a campaign to reeducate the nation brought changes more quickly than many had thought possible.

By the end of the decade polls showed that a majority of Americans supported equal pay for men and women, and approved of women in political office. They believed that women should have equal access to educational opportunity, and many approved of abortion in certain cases. There was a growing realization that men should share equally in raising children, and that discrimination on the basis of sex should be prohibited.

Language itself was affected by the consciousness-raising of both women and men. The term "Ms." was a joke when it was first proposed. By the end of the seventies, it was commonplace in business usage. The substitution of "person" for "man" in compounds such as "chairman" sounded strange when it was first used. It too became commonplace, and many other terms implying males, such as "mailman," were changed to neuter constructions such as "mail carrier." Many women began to keep their birth names after marriage.

(29)

There were victories for women in the courts and in the legislature. The decade opened with the first formal charges of sex discrimination against a federally-funded institution, the University of Maryland. The Supreme Court ruled in 1971 that companies could not refuse to hire women with small children unless the same policy applied to men. These were only the first of many sex discrimination suits, including one that compelled Little League baseball teams to permit girls to join.

The women's movement lobbied Congress into passing the Equal Rights Amendment in 1972. It had first been introduced in 1923. Yet after many states ratified the amendment, opposition to it grew. Those opposing it claimed among other things that it would nullify benefits that women were entitled to under law, such as being exempt from serving in the armed forces. When the deadline for ratification approached with little chance of the amendment securing the required two-thirds approval of the states, Congress in 1978 extended the deadline for ratification to June 30, 1982.

There were many milestones for women's progress in the seventies. In 1970 the first woman general—Anna Mae Hays—was commissioned in the army. In 1972 Shirley Chisholm, a black Congressperson from Brooklyn, waged a campaign for nomination for president. In 1974 the Merchant Marine Academy admitted women for the first time, followed later by the Army, Navy, and Air Force academies. In Connecticut, Ella Grasso won election as governor in 1974—the first woman governor not riding on the coattails of her husband. The following year, the first women's bank was opened. The first United States women astronauts were selected in 1978.

Organized religion was also affected. The first woman Lutheran minister—Elizabeth A. Platz—was ordained in 1970. Two years later, Sally Preisand became the first woman rabbi in the United States. Eleven women were ordained priests in the Episcopal church, although the hierarchy did not recognize them.

The most controversial of the women's issues was abortion. In 1973 the Supreme Court forbade the government to interfere in early abortion (the first three months), knocking down many state laws against abortion. The decision caused a furor. While organizations such as the National Organization for Women (NOW) acclaimed it, other groups organized to support a constitutional amendment

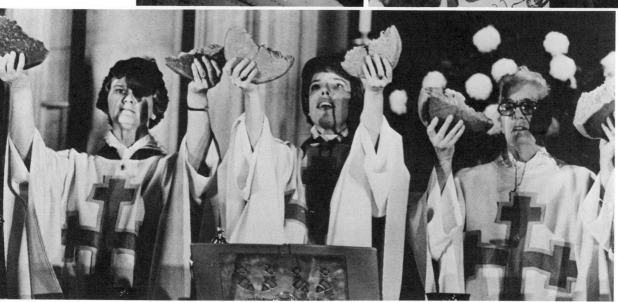

Top left: First-Lieutenant Jessica Grafola, seen here doing preflight checks, was the first female pilot to fly the Chinook helicopter. Top right: the most controversial women's issue was abortion. Here, a 1979 march in Boston in support of a woman's right to choose an abortion. Below: the first women of the U.S. Episcopal Church to perform publicly the priestly acts of the Eucharist service. Left to right: Rev. Allison Cheek, Rev. Carter Heyward, and Rev. Jeannette Piccard.

Civil rights protests shifted to the north in the
1970s. In this Pulitzer Prize-winning photo of
racial disturbances in Boston, a black passerby
was attacked by a white mob with an American flag.

against abortion. Rallying under the name "Right to Life," they became a special interest group of unusual intensity and dedication. The Right to Life groups strongly lobbied to withdraw all public funds that would pay for abortion for the poor. The decade ended with the issue yet undecided.

Civil Rights

In the 1960s the civil rights movement won basic legal and voting rights for blacks and other racial minorities. The fight was centered mainly in southern states. In the 1970s the focus of the civil rights movement changed to a drive for equality in jobs, housing, and education, and the area of conflict shifted to the north. The consensus that had been forged in the marches and boycotts of the sixties was broken. Busing to achieve racial equality in schools was a controversial issue, although the Supreme Court upheld it as a legal way to ensure desegregation. In older cities, where the inner cities contained a greater percentage of minorities, busing often sparked violent protests.

Affirmative action, the policy of giving minority applicants special consideration in hiring, admission to schools, and promotion, was another heated issue. Many called it reverse discrimination. In the Bakke decision of 1978, the Supreme Court struck down the use of rigid quotas in accepting minority applicants, but approved of affirmative action programs and said that race could be a factor in the choosing of candidates for medical school.

Clear-cut advances for blacks came with a tremendous increase in black elected officials, especially at the state and local levels. President Carter claimed that he appointed more minority citizens as judges than all previous presidents combined.

Homosexuals also "came out of the closet" and demanded freedom from discrimination. Gay Liberation produced some successes in areas such as San Francisco, but failed in other places. In Dade County, Florida, citizens voted down a resolution to protect homosexuals from discrimination in employment, housing, and public accommodations.

The fastest-growing minority in the United States was still struggling for equal rights. Latin Americans numbered from twelve to

(33)

sixteen million, most of them centered in the southwest, Florida, and New York. Illegal immigrants and high birth rates swelled their numbers, but as a group their political clout was still weak. They did not vote in large numbers.

The Bicentennial

The two-hundredth birthday of the United States was the occasion for a spectacular celebration. It was a day to count blessings and, after years of Vietnam and Watergate, to celebrate what was good about the country. President Ford said Americans should "break out the flag, strike up the band, light up the sky," and the country did. In parades and fireworks in countless small communities, and in spectacular pageants in large cities, the country had itself a fine time.

Perhaps the most spectacular celebration was New York's "Tall Ships" regatta. Old-fashioned sailing ships from many nations gathered in New York Harbor amid a gala fireworks display at the Statue of Liberty. Sailing up the Hudson River, the ships formed a line miles long as millions of people lined the banks. There were sixteen "tall ships" in Operation Sail, as well as thirty thousand smaller craft.

The Bicentennial year was also a presidential election year. The Democratic nomination was captured by Jimmy Carter, a former governor of Georgia who was unknown outside his area of the country. He promised to give the country "a government as good as its people," and ran on the slogan "Why not the best?" Opposing him was the first unelected president in the country's history, Gerald R. Ford. For the first time since 1960, presidential debates were a feature of the campaign. In a close election, with a turnout of only 54 percent of eligible voters, Carter won.

Religion and Cults

Religion played a great part in American life in the seventies. With the election of Jimmy Carter, who described himself as a "born-again Christian," there seemed to be a new awareness of fundamentalist Christianity.

The Bicentennial was a happy high point of the decade. Above: President Gerald R. Ford prepares to ring a ceremonial bell on an American aircraft carrier participating in festivities in New York Harbor. Above right: the Polish full-rigged ship *Dar Pomorza* taking part in the Operation Sail Bicentennial celebration. Right: children, holding some of the many flags that have flown over the United States, took part in the Bicentennial celebration.

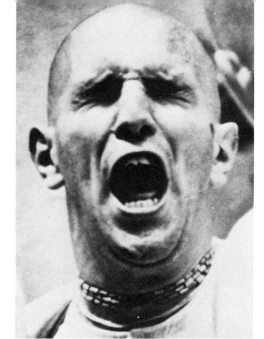

Right: the Hare Krishna movement, one of whose members is shown here, was a highly visible cult because of its members' practice of dancing and chanting in the streets of large cities.

One of the major religious events of the decade was the visit of Pope John Paul II to the United States in 1979. He was met with great enthusiasm as he traveled 11,500 miles, giving forty-nine speeches, prayers, and homilies, before being received at the White House by President Carter.

Many Americans were drawn to Eastern religions such as Zen Buddhism and Hinduism. Others turned to cults, which often had Eastern religious influence. Among these was the Hare Krishna movement, whose middle-class American members shaved their heads, put on pastel-colored robes, and marched through city streets chanting and selling literature. More conventionally attired were the youthful members of the Unification Church, dubbed "Moonies" because of their devotion to the South Korean Reverend Sun Myung Moon. Some cults amassed a great deal of money from the voluntary work of their members, and bought into businesses and real estate. The Moonies even published their own daily newspaper. The most bizarre and tragic of the cults was that headed by the Reverend Jim Jones, who founded his People's Temple in California, where he had ties with many local politicians. Led by Jones, the group moved to a remote section of the South American country of Guyana.

In 1978 California Congressman Leo Ryan went to investigate the commune that Jones and his devotees had built in the jungle. Ryan and four other people with him were killed by Temple members. Soon afterward, Jones ordered his followers to commit suicide. Sitting on a white throne, he presided as babies and children were given grape-flavored drinks laced with cyanide. Then the adults took the potion. More than nine hundred were found dead, along with their leader, who had a bullet in his head. America's reaction of shock and horror led to demands for closer scrutiny and control of cults.

The fervor of "born-again Christians" was among the religious phenomena of the decade. In the series of photographs opposite (middle of page), two girls overcome with emotion emerge from baptismal waters and embrace friends. Lower left: the followers of Rev. Sun Myung Moon's Unification Church remove posters that were put up to publicize the sect's "Bicentennial God Bless America" rally at Yankee Stadium. Accused of defacing the city with their posters, followers obligingly removed them after the rally. Lower right: Pope John Paul II was the first pope to be received at the White House.

(37)

The Me Generation

In the turmoil of the sixties, the energy of America seemed to focus on political movements—civil rights and the struggle for peace. In the seventies, almost as if in reaction to the outer-directed sixties, the nation began a search for personal fulfillment and self-discovery. The popularity of Eastern religions and disciplines was one of the results of the national concern with self. Yoga was popular not only as a means of exercise but as a guide to a better life.

Psychological treatments meant to bring out the authentic, wonderful person inside us all contributed their names to the language. People were Rolfed, Ested, went to Esalen, took up scientology, or learned Eastern martial arts—all to develop their inner selves. "Getting your head together" was the theme of a decade that hoped to master the secret of life in two weekends in a hotel.

Fads, Styles, and Gadgets

Fashions of the decade were decidedly mixed. The end of the mini-skirt came early in the decade, but the heralded maxi failed to catch on. For a brief season hot pants (ultra-short shorts) worn with boots was the style. Later came the layered look, a combination of several sweaters, blouses, and jackets worn over each other.

The fashion staple of the decade really was jeans. They took on the role of a uniform, along with the ubiquitous T-shirt, often emblazoned with a slogan meant to be humorous, passionate, political, or obscene. Smart designers soon realized that the need for fashion status could be satisfied by stitching a name-label on the rear pocket of ordinary jeans, along with a tighter cut. Designer jeans, at twice or three times the price of ordinary, durable jeans without the extra label, were a smash success.

Almost as popular was the runner's outfit of split-leg shorts, sweat band, T-shirt, and running shoes. Running was touted as the solution for all sorts of health problems as well as a help to a happy life and a better self-image. Stores selling nothing but running gear appeared, and millions bought books that told them how and why to run. America showed its talent for ballyhooing a simple activity into a business.

Above: Yoga became popular as an aid to health, fitness, and serenity of mind; as a fad, running prompted the sale of books and all sorts of running gear. Left: jeans were the most popular costume of the decade. This poster showed New York Ranger hockey players promoting the fad.

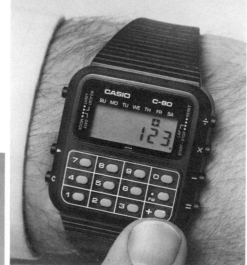

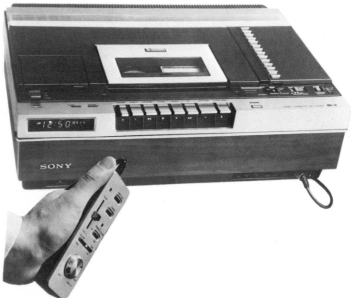

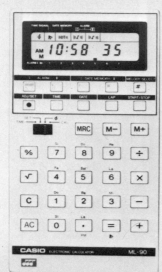

Other fads ranged from the ridiculous to . . . the more ridiculous. One Christmas, the pet rock appeared. Nothing more than a rock packaged in a miniature pet carryall with tongue-in-cheek instructions for care and play, the pet rock became a prime example of conspicuous consumption—money spent for its own sake. Mood rings contained a stone that was supposed to change color along with the wearer's mood. Then there was the drink of the decade—Perrier water. Nothing more than soda water imported from France, it had two qualities that made it a success: it cost a lot and it wasn't fattening.

If a modern Rip Van Winkle had fallen asleep at the beginning of the decade and awoke on December 31, 1979, the first thing he would have noticed would have been a variety of electronic gadgets that had not been there before but were now commonplace. Hand calculators sold for ten dollars or less and threatened to do away with the need for multiplication tables. Digital watches and clocks, games that were played on home TV screens, video tape recorders, even home computers were all part of the electronics revolution of the seventies.

Digital watches, some priced as low as $10, became another rage. Many models crammed onto the tiny face not only the time, but also the date, month, day of the week, and, as in the model shown (upper right), calculator functions as well. The video tape recorder enabled television viewers to tape their favorite shows while they were out of the house or watching another program. Shown here (below digital watch) is the Sony Betamax. Electronic games that used the television screen as a playing board were another electronic hit, as were calculators, which became almost indispensable to businesses and individuals alike. CB radios, with which a motorist could communicate with other cars similarly equipped, became so popular that the CBer's code vocabulary became part of the national jargon. And, meanwhile, the golden arches of McDonald's signaled the availability of the "Big Mac," one of the most popular foods of the decade.

(41)

A CHANGING WORLD

The seventies was a turbulent decade which saw the birth of new nations, the overthrow of governments, and a shift in the post–World War II alliances. The United States and China came to a mutual recognition that solidified the split between the two Communist giants, China and the USSR. At the same time, the struggle for shrinking world resources strained America's alliance with western Europe and Japan, whose rapidly growing economies brought them into competition with the United States.

The third world, which includes many developing nations of Africa, Asia, and South America, used its numbers and resources to gain an increasing say in world affairs. The OPEC nations showed surprising strength in increasing the price of petroleum, vital to the economies of the developed nations. Yet the gap between rich and poor nations continued, with the spectacle of mass starvation in many places contrasting with the high standards of living in the industrialized countries.

Threats to world peace were heightened by nuclear proliferation. India exploded its first nuclear bomb in 1974 after diverting nuclear fuel from its domestic energy needs. Pakistan was rumored to be building a bomb of its own. In many nations, terrorists showed their ability to disrupt the affairs of a nation even though they had the support of only a tiny minority of the population.

China

Since the Communist takeover in 1949, the United States had refused to recognize China's regime on the mainland, claiming that the Nationalist government on the offshore island of Taiwan represented all of China. But there was a hint of change in early 1971, when an American table tennis team was permitted to accept China's invitation to visit the country. The media called it "ping-pong diplomacy."

Left: although the United States disengaged from Vietnam, the horror of war and its aftermath continued. Vietnamese refugees fled throughout Southeast Asia. Some, with a boat their only home, became known as "boat people." Top right: a new nation, Bangladesh, was born out of conflict between India and Pakistan in 1971. Formerly known as East Pakistan, Bangladesh was the scene of starvation and misery. Lower right: the great development in foreign policy of the seventies was the establishment of ties between the United States and the People's Republic of China. President and Mrs. Nixon here tour the Great Wall of China.

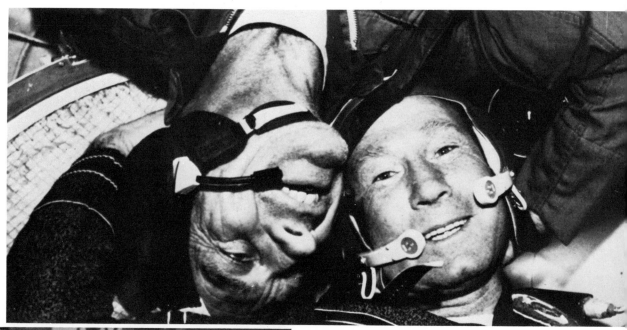

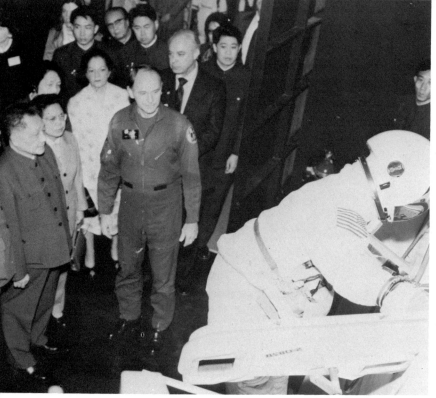

Above: *détente*'s most concrete symbol was the joint U.S.-USSR manned satellite docking in earth orbit. Shown are Soviet cosmonaut Aleksei A. Leonov and American astronaut Donald K. Slayton in the orbiter module. Left: Chinese Vice-Premier Deng Xiaoping visited the United States in 1979. One of the stops on his tour was the Johnson Space Center in Houston, Texas, shown here as he and his wife were briefed by astronaut Alan L. Bean.

That summer, President Nixon's National Security Adviser, Henry Kissinger, dropped out of sight while on a trip to Pakistan. Reporters were told he was ill, but he had secretly flown to China for exploratory talks with Prime Minister Chou En-lai. Not long afterward, Nixon astonished the nation with the announcement that he had accepted a Chinese offer to visit the People's Republic.

Nixon's trip, in February of 1972, was heavily covered by American newspapers and television. After meeting Mao, sightseeing, and exchanging numerous banquet toasts, Nixon and Chou issued a joint statement called the Shanghai Communiqué. Formal relations were not yet established, but agreement was reached on liaison offices in both countries' capitals.

The new relationship was based on the increasing hostility between China and the Soviet Union. Nixon and Kissinger believed a relationship with China would help the United States obtain concessions from the Soviets and speed American disengagement from Vietnam.

It was thought that the U.S. and China would soon establish full relations, but Watergate and other matters kept Nixon and, later, President Ford from taking the final step. Finally President Carter, at the end of 1978, announced full recognition of the People's Republic as the legal representative of China. Relations with Taiwan were reduced to a private level.

Détente

Nixon's and Kissinger's plan to build "a new order of peace" called for an improvement in American relations with the Soviet Union. This relaxation of tensions known as *détente* began in the early 1970s. Increased trade relations led to talks on arms control, and the first SALT (Strategic Arms Limitation Treaty) was signed in 1972.

During Ford's administration, *détente* began to fade. Soviet interference in Africa caused some conservatives to call *détente* a one-way street, and it was scarcely mentioned in the Republican platform of 1976.

When Jimmy Carter became president, he instituted a policy of encouraging human rights, embarrassing the Soviet Union because of its repressive policy toward dissidents and refusal to let citizens emigrate. After a rocky start, Carter's Administration succeeded in negotiating a second SALT treaty. It was signed by Carter and Soviet Premier Leonid Brezhnev in 1979, but ratification in the U.S. Senate was delayed. The Soviet invasion of Afghanistan in December 1979 killed *détente* and ruined chances for Senate ratification of SALT II.

The Middle East

The source of much of the world's imported oil, the Middle East remained an unstable trouble spot during the decade. In October 1973, seeking to regain territory lost during the Six-Day War of 1967, Egypt and Syria swept into Israeli-held territory in the Sinai Peninsula and the Golan Heights. But the Israelis rallied and took back the disputed territory. Cease-fires were established on October 22 and 23, and for the next two years Henry Kissinger practiced "shuttle diplomacy," flying between Tel Aviv and Arab capitals to mediate the dispute.

A major surprise breaking the deadlock was the visit of Egyptian President Anwar el-Sadat to Jerusalem in 1977. This was the first time an Arab leader had visited the Jewish state since its founding in 1948. The following year, when talks between Israel and Egypt lagged, President Carter invited Sadat and Israeli Prime Minister Menachem Begin to meet with him. After eleven secluded days at the presidential retreat at Camp David, the men emerged with the announcement of an agreement. A peace treaty was formally signed at the White House on March 31, 1979.

A major failure of American policy in the Middle East was the revolution that overthrew the Shah of Iran in January 1979. Heavily supplied by the United States to serve as the "policemen" in the oil-rich Persian Gulf area, the Shah's forces were unable to quell mass demonstrations against the Shah's harsh regime. He was replaced by a fanatic religious leader, the Ayatollah Ruhollah Khomeini, who had been in exile in Paris. The Ayatollah exhibited an intense hatred for the United States and its interference in Iranian affairs, and on November 4, 1979, militant followers of his seized the American Embassy in Teheran and took prisoner its American staff members. Faced with a situation in which the use of force was likely to harm the hostages, the United States felt frustrated as seldom before.

(46)

Above: the war between Israel and the Arab nations of Egypt and Syria in October 1973 led to the Arab oil embargo. Below: the signing of the Israeli-Egyptian peace treaty at the White House on March 26, 1979. Left to right: Egyptian President Anwar el-Sadat, President Jimmy Carter, and Israeli Prime Minister Menachem Begin.

Right: a five-year drought in the early seventies plagued the Sahel, a zone of Africa just south of the Sahara Desert. Some 1,200 square miles were denuded of vegetation, resulting in human starvation, the destruction of herds of animals, and widespread malnutrition affecting much of the population.

Above left: young Sandinista guerrilla fighters at a barricade in Nicaragua during the insurrection that overthrew Anastasio Somoza in 1979. Above right: the Union of South Africa remained frozen in its *apartheid* policies of separation of the races. Bloody riots in Soweto, a black enclave, erupted when police fired on black high school students in the segregated township near Johannesburg.

Africa and Latin America

The decade saw the end of the civil war in Nigeria and the liberation of Mozambique and Angola from Portuguese colonial rule. In Uganda, the repressive dictatorship of Idi Amin was overthrown.

American concern over Russian and Cuban intervention in Mozambique and Angola led Secretary of State Kissinger to urge the United States to support an opposing counterforce. That was in 1975, when the United States had just left the disastrous involvement in Vietnam, and Congress forbade a commitment in Africa. Further turmoil in the Horn of Africa—the northeast corner of the continent—brought renewed American interest. Ethiopia accepted Russian aid, and the Americans established a presence in Somalia, Ethiopia's southern neighbor.

In southern Africa, encouraging progress was made toward a peaceful conciliation of the ruling minority whites and the black majority. In Rhodesia, Britain, with U.S. support, was able to bring the several sides in the armed conflict to the conference table. The Union of South Africa continued its *apartheid* policies, and growing protests by blacks increased the tensions in one of the world's mineral-rich areas.

The American relationship with South America erupted into scandal as the Senate hearings on CIA activities confirmed U.S. secret actions to control South American governments. To many, one of the worst abuses was CIA use of organized crime to attempt the assassination of Cuban leader Fidel Castro.

In Chile in 1970 Salvador Allende became the first South American Marxist to win leadership of his country in a free election. It was later revealed that the CIA and the multinational corporation ITT conspired to prevent his election. In September 1973 Allende died in a military coup against his government, and General Augustin Pinochet became dictator of the country. Many thought the CIA had played a role in Pinochet's seizure of power.

The Carter Administration sought to encourage democratic regimes in South America. Carter's policy was tested in Nicaragua, where one of the United States's most faithful allies, right-wing dictator Anastasio Somoza, was threatened by a leftist uprising led by Sandinista guerrillas. Carter refused to intervene as Nicaraguan popular support shifted to the Sandinistas, and Somoza was overthrown.

(49)

THE WORLD OF SCIENCE

Science and technology had an ambivalent image in the seventies. Environmentalists, conservationists, and others often saw technology as the enemy of human life. It was clear that science had a greater effect on people's lives than ever before, and the average citizen demanded a voice in the making of scientific decisions. An accident at the nuclear energy plant at Three Mile Island near Harrisburg, Pennsylvania, heightened fears that technology was out of control and threatened our health and lives. Additional concern was voiced over the possibility of an accident in the genetic research laboratories where scientists were experimenting with the elements of life itself. Nevertheless, the decade saw many scientific advances of major scope.

In physics, work continued in the search for the basic structure of matter. The most famous discovery was the proof of the existence of the quark. Thought by some to be the basic element of matter, a quark is a particle that is the building block of protons and neutrons in the nucleus of the atom. Speculation continued over the question of whether there might be something yet smaller than a quark.

New discoveries in astronomy were made through the use of satellites carrying instruments above the distortion of the earth's atmosphere. The decade saw the mathematical verification of what was once thought of as a bizarre theory—the existence of "black holes." These were objects of such great gravity that they could suck in whole stars. Even light could not escape from the grip of a black hole; hence they are invisible and detectible only by their effect on visible matter.

Although none of the decade's achievements in space captured the attention of Americans as much as the landing of the first men on the moon in 1969, exploration of nearby planets produced spectacular scientific information. Probes to Mercury, Venus, Jupiter, and Saturn, and the Viking landings on Mars brought more information about Earth's neighbors than in all of previous human history.

(50)

More space exploration took place in the seventies than ever before. Left: a Skylab 3 crewman performs an extravehicular activity. Right: the Skylab 2 space station, with Earth and a star rising above the horizon in the background. The Skylab's return to Earth in 1979 and subsequent disintegration in the atmosphere caused worldwide concern as to where the pieces might hit. Fortunately, they landed near Perth, Australia, in a desert area, and no one was harmed.

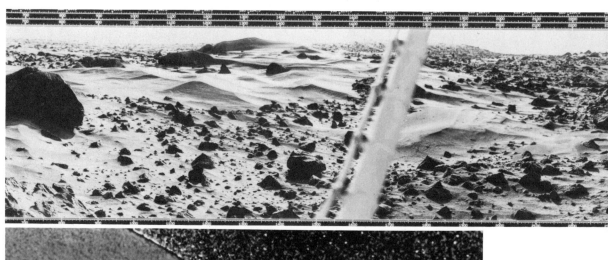

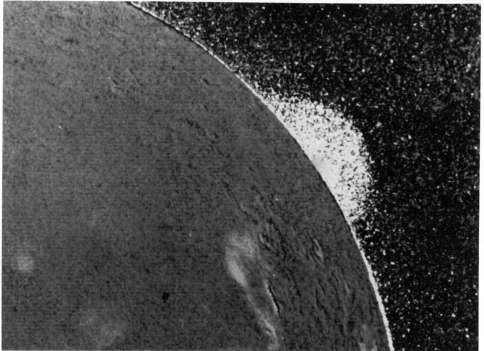

Top: a spectacular view of the landscape of Mars, taken from the Viking I lander on August 3, 1976. Bottom: this picture shows an erupting volcano on Io, one of Jupiter's moons, photographed by Voyager I during its flyby of Jupiter in March 1979. Opposite: Jupiter and its four largest moons, called the Galilean satellites, were photographed individually by Voyager I and assembled into this collage.

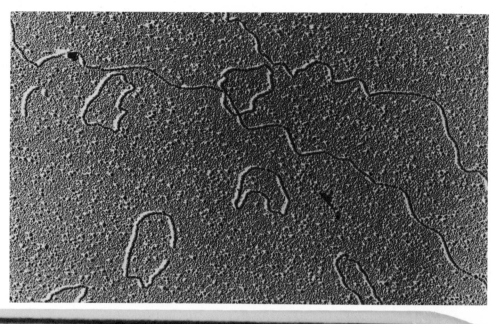

Top: viewed through an electron microscope is a recombinant
DNA molecule, stretching from upper left to lower right.
The smaller rings are normal DNA molecules. Bottom: the
MAC-4 one-chip computer is compared to a standard-sized
paper clip. The chip's numerous functional areas are labeled.

Before space travel could be a reality, it was necessary to prove that humans could survive in space for extended periods of time. In 1973 Skylab astronauts Pete Conrad, Joseph Kerwin, and Paul Weitz stayed twenty-eight days in the orbiting Skylab 100-ton space station. The experiment showed the potential for prolonged human stays in space. Skylab's sensitive instruments also increased human knowledge about the earth and sun. Earth photographs charted storms in the Pacific, and pictures of the sun revealed a violence of activity never seen before.

The most controversial scientific developments of the decade were in the field of biology. Biologists had been studying the chemical DNA (deoxyribonucleic acid), the carrier of the genetic code. That code determines whether an individual is male or female, white or black, brown-eyed or blue-eyed, and ultimately whether an individual has the characteristics of a human, a frog, or a plant.

But in the seventies a technology was discovered that could actually redesign the DNA molecule. By cutting up the molecule and combining bits from different organisms, scientists were able to rearrange life at its most fundamental level. The discovery aroused fears that scientists would inadvertently develop dangerous microbes that would then breed out of control. The debate over control of DNA research continued into the 1980s. But creation of new organisms held out great possibilities for industry and medicine.

Tampering with the natural order was symbolized most graphically when the first "test-tube baby" was born on July 25, 1978. Her name was Louise Joy Brown. She was conceived in a glass dish in an English laboratory and implanted in her mother's womb. Religious groups were among those who debated the implications of this kind of scientific power.

To the average person, the most noticeable technological changes in daily life were in electronics. The development of the semiconductor silicon chip resulted in many everyday products from home computers to pocket calculators and video games. Two decades before, the transistor had seemed a marvel of miniaturization; but now a silicon chip the size of a match tip can contain circuitry equivalent to sixty-eight thousand transistor switches. With mass production, the price of silicon chips fell drastically, and electronics became the chief industry whose products decreased in price in the inflationary seventies.

(55)

SCREEN, STAGE, ART, AND BOOKS

Movies and Theater

The movie industry emphasized the "blockbuster" in the seventies. The trend was toward higher prices, greater advertising, and, in the case of a movie that achieved blockbuster success, one or more sequels to capitalize on that success. Some movies grossed over one hundred million dollars in admissions. Among the notable successes of the decade were *The Godfather* (parts one and two), *Jaws, Star Wars, Rocky, Saturday Night Fever,* and *Close Encounters of the Third Kind.* Some of the sequels—notably *Jaws II* and *Rocky, Part II*—did not achieve the success of the originals, but the producer of *Star Wars* announced its place as the fourth in a series of nine projected movies.

There were movies of more moderate success that dealt with current problems. These included *Taxi Driver* and *Nashville,* which were about the causes of irrational violence. *All the President's Men* was an account of the breaking of the Watergate story, with superstars Robert Redford and Dustin Hoffman playing the parts of the *Washington Post* reporters Bob Woodward and Carl Bernstein. The Vietnam War was the subject of several notable movies: *Coming Home, The Deer Hunter,* and *Apocalypse Now.*

One of the movie blockbusters of the decade was *Jaws,* the story of a resort town threatened by a great white shark.

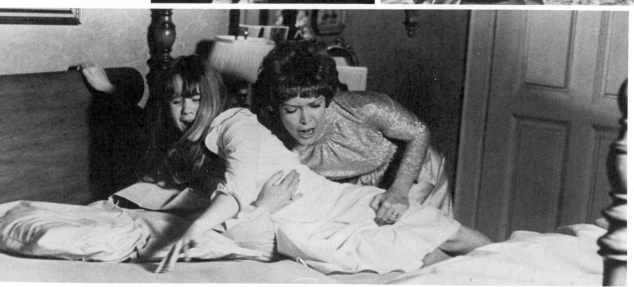

Top left: Marlon Brando supposedly wanted the title role in *The Godfather* so badly that he was willing to take a screen test to get it. Top right: Woody Allen's characteristic movie-making style was most popular in the bittersweet *Annie Hall,* which starred Diane Keaton, shown here with Allen in a scene from the film. Bottom: *The Exorcist* started a string of pictures about children who were possessed by evil. In the original, shown here, Linda Blair played a girl possessed by a demon; Ellen Burstyn played her mother.

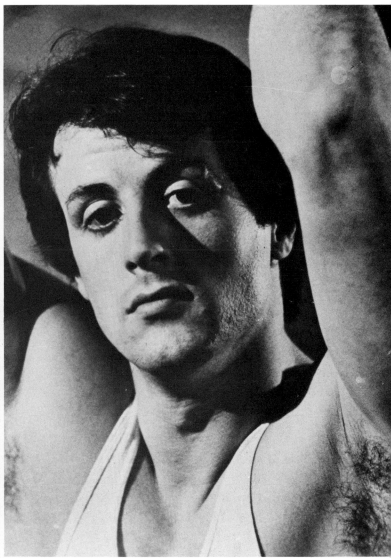

Left: John Travolta's electricity as a performer and the songs of the Bee Gees helped to make disco and the movie *Saturday Night Fever* big hits. Above: Sylvester Stallone both wrote and starred in *Rocky*, the saga of an amateur boxer who challenged the heavyweight champion of the world.

Star Wars, the biggest movie hit of all time, started a science-fiction boom. Some thought the most interesting characters in the film were the two robots. Shown here, momentarily in trouble, is R2-D2.

One of the surprises of the blockbuster movies was that they brought to the forefront of the movie business several young American directors such as Francis Ford Coppola, Martin Scorsese, Steven Spielberg, and George Lucas. The new directors used their sudden success to take creative control of their new projects, and some foresaw a change in movies Hollywood offered its public.

The old-fashioned escape film continued to prosper, in traditional format such as the love story titled *Love Story,* and in disaster films that found their greatest popularity in the beginning of the decade. These included *Airport, Earthquake,* and *The Towering Inferno.* Action found an outlet in the craze for oriental culture in the kung fu movies of Bruce Lee in the early seventies. Nostalgia was also popular, especially for the 1950s, in such films as *Grease* and *American Graffiti.*

The biggest genre of the decade was the horror–science fiction film. Horror reached an apex with *The Exorcist,* a movie that prompted not only a sequel but also many copies starring "evil" children. Science fiction, a dormant Hollywood genre since the fifties, was revivified in new ways after the success of *Star Wars.*

Both blacks and women made inroads into the movie business as producer-directors, and by providing serious themes. Movies with strong women themes included *A Woman Under the Influence, The Turning Point,* and *An Unmarried Woman.* Movies made strictly for a black audience, called "blaxploitation" films, drew large audiences. Serious black actors such as Sidney Poitier and James Earl Jones were playing the kind of lead roles previously reserved for whites.

Live theater prospered as never before. The number of professional theaters in the United States quadrupled in the seventies. Theater's heart, New York's Broadway, broke its all-time box office record by selling more than $100 million worth of tickets in a single season. Joseph Papp, the creative force behind the New York Shakespeare Festival, introduced to Broadway many important productions and new playwrights such as David Rabe. The biggest hit of the decade was Michael Bennett's *A Chorus Line,* which looked behind the scenes at the lives of show business dancers. The ever-popular comedy writer Neil Simon continued his string of hits. Around the country, regional theaters grew in importance as originators of plays that came to national attention. Black theater and British imports were also popular during the decade.

Television

The seventies saw a reaction against the generally low level of network television. People questioned the effect long hours of television watching were having on young people. At the same time, public or educational television stations found greater popularity with British imports and with programming that originated in the United States. In the cities where they were available, cable television and pay-TV brought a large choice of programming.

Network television scored its greatest successes in news and sports broadcasting, both of which were augmented by technical innovations. Portable minicameras enabled news reporters to get to the scene and record events as they happened. Instant replay, slow motion, and stop motion were among the many techniques used by sports television coverage that made a seat at home a better place to watch a game than a seat at the event itself. Satellite broadcasts opened up the world to events as they were happening, and video cassette recorders allowed viewers to tape programs for replay.

Television often influenced the events it covered. The effect of viewing the Vietnam War from one's living room may have played a role in encouraging resistance to the war. Watergate became a soap opera for many people who came home from work to watch replays of the hearings of the Senate and House committees investigating it. Sports and political events were tailored to the needs of television. The phenomenon reached a height with the coverage of the hostage situation in Iran.

In entertainment programming, the most significant development was the introduction of realistic situation comedies which took current events as a topic. The most popular program of the decade was "All in the Family," which featured a bigoted resident of Queens, New York, Archie Bunker, and his family. The show's producer, Norman Lear, continued with a series of hits based on characters that first appeared in "All in the Family." Lear was first to produce a series that featured a black family, "The Jeffersons." Another popular series that resulted in spin-offs was "The Mary Tyler Moore Show," which reflected social concerns in the life of a young single working woman. Crime and police stories were popular, as always, with the twist that several featured women as the main characters. Nostalgia for the 1950s also found a place on television in the series "Happy Days."

(62)

Left: "Stifle your-self, Edith!" was one of Archie Bunker's (Carroll O'Connor) familiar lines in the comedy series "All in the Family." Below: wearing a black leather jacket is Henry Winkler playing Arthur Fonza-relli ("The Fonz") in the nostalgia series "Happy Days."

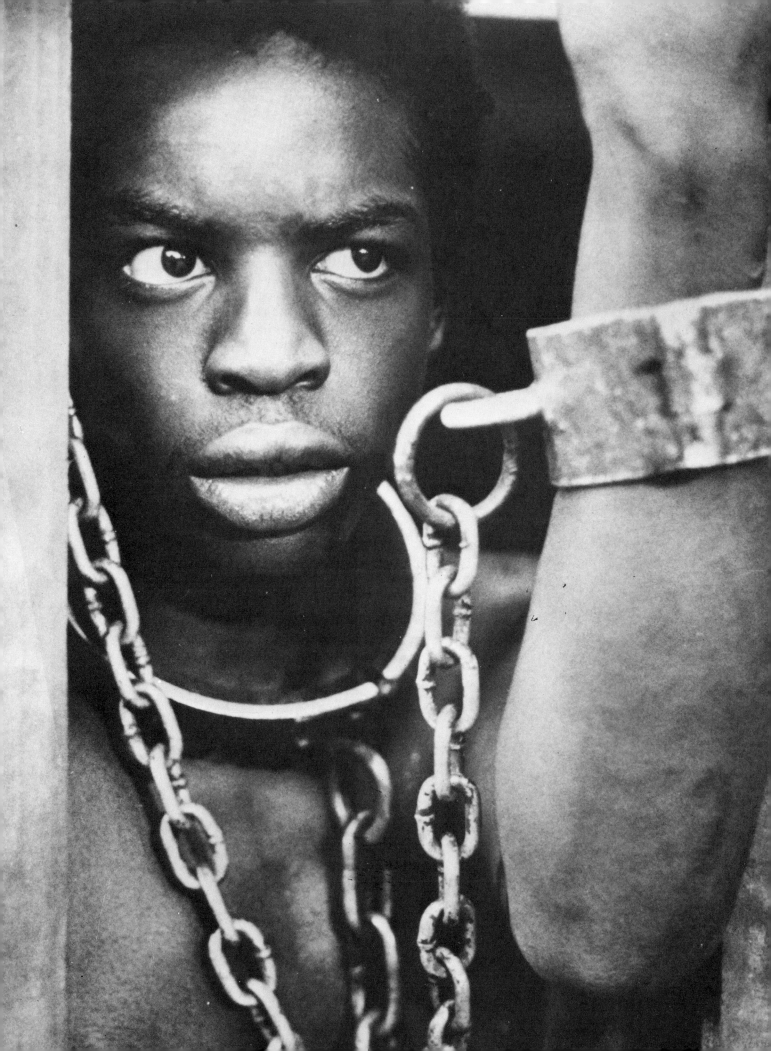

A new way of scheduling programs was the miniseries, which told a continuing story in several parts shown on successive nights. Originally used by public television for imported British series, the technique was taken up by the networks. The most popular program in television history was the miniseries "Roots," which attracted an audience of one hundred thirty million when it was first shown in 1977. Another popular miniseries was "Holocaust."

Innovations introduced by public television were not limited to scheduling. Its superb children's programs such as "Sesame Street" used TV techniques to educate as well as entertain. The public television system brought opera, ballet, theater, and concerts to millions who had never seen them on a stage. In 1973 PBS took viewers in their own living rooms into the living room of another American family. In a series of documentaries, the real life of a California family, the Louds, was filmed and televised.

Music and Dance

There was no superstar in popular music in the seventies to equal the Beatles in the sixties or Elvis Presley in the fifties. Instead, popular music became fragmented into different types, each with its own brand of devotees. Punk rock, heavy metal, new wave, and disco all had origins in the rock music of the previous two decades.

Perhaps the most significant of the new forms of popular music was disco. A blend of rock and Latin beats such as Jamaican reggae and salsa, disco music combined a compelling rhythm with less important lyrics. It was meant to be danced to, and it spawned many disco clubs, the most famous of which was New York's Studio 54, where flashing lights emphasized the beat of the music. Donna Summer with "Bad Girl" and the Bee Gees with "Stayin' Alive" were among the most popular of the disco artists.

The TV miniseries "Roots" began with the story of Kunta Kinte (LeVar Burton), who was brought to America as a slave. This series was based on the book by Alex Haley.

Above: "Sesame Street," produced by the Children's Television Workshop for the Public Broadcasting System, featured live characters and the Muppets of Jim Henson. Ernie and Bert, the Cookie Monster, Grover, and the Count were known to millions of American children. Left: shows produced by the British Broadcasting Company often offered better writing and acting than American network programming. Appearing in the United States on the Public Broadcasting System (PBS) were such British shows as "Upstairs, Downstairs," whose cast is shown here.

Above: considered part of "heavy metal" rock, the group Kiss drew young fans with unconventional costumes and by never permitting publicity photographs of themselves without makeup. Left: Elton John mugged and clowned his way to superstardom as a singer. With lyricist Bernie Taupin, he wrote most of his own songs, generally light and clever lyrics with a mild rock sound.

Opera too had its superstars, such as tenor Luciano Pavarotti and soprano Beverly Sills, who were nearly as famous as their popular music counterparts. The number of opera houses increased and the number of symphony orchestras doubled.

Ballet was another of the arts given a boost by television exposure. Russian defectors Mikhail Baryshnikov and Natalia Makarova heightened the public's awareness of ballet. The number of dance companies around the country increased tenfold during the decade. Modern dance prospered too, with important companies led by Martha Graham, Merce Cunningham, and Twyla Tharp.

Art

The cultural boom resulted in the creation of more than two hundred new museums in the decade. From 1977 to 1979 the King Tut exhibition of treasures from ancient Egypt toured the country, drawing enormous crowds wherever it went.

Pablo Picasso, perhaps the greatest twentieth century artist, died during the decade, inspiring a retrospective of his long and immensely productive career. Inflation touched off skyrocketing prices for works of art, prized for their investment value. Such American moderns as Jackson Pollock and David Smith were among those whose works brought astronomical prices at auction.

Books

The publishing world saw a great increase in the number of books sold and the tremendous amounts offered to authors for paperback or movie rights to their books. Many worried that this trend would produce a tiny group of superstar authors and squeeze the moderately successful book out of the marketplace.

How-to books were among the most popular of the decade. Americans were told how to grow houseplants, cook, invest, diet, improve their homes, and get their heads together. Books that capitalized on sudden crazes, such as Jim Fixx's *Book of Running,* were found at the top of best-seller lists.

In serious literature, two Americans—both immigrants—won the Nobel Prize for fiction. Saul Bellow, from Canada, taught at the University of Chicago. Isaac Bashevis Singer, a Polish refugee, wrote in Yiddish about the scenes of his youth in Poland.

Left: Isaac Bashevis Singer won the Nobel Prize for Literature for his short stories and novels written in Yiddish and translated into English. Below left: opera star Beverly Sills as Violetta in *La Traviata*. In her numerous concert and television appearances, Ms. Sills did much to spread opera's popularity. Below right: Mikhail Baryshnikov's looks and his ability to almost defy gravity in his dancing made him the best-known ballet figure of the decade.

A shadow fell over the sports world when an Arab commando group seized the Israeli team headquarters at the Olympic village in Munich. A masked terrorist appears on the balcony of the village building where Israeli athletes were held hostage. In a shootout with West German police, the terrorists killed eleven Israeli hostages.

SPORTS, ON AND OFF THE FIELD

The world of sport is normally confined to the playing field. Within that artificial world, the seventies saw many achievements. Among them: Hank Aaron broke Babe Ruth's lifetime home run record; Muhammad Ali recovered his title as heavyweight champion of the world; Jack Nicklaus won eight major-tournament victories in golf; and O. J. Simpson gained over two thousand yards rushing in a single professional football season.

Increasingly, however, the sports world was invaded by the disruptive influences of the real world. Palestinian terrorists violated the sanctuary of the international Olympic village at Munich, Germany, in 1972 and killed Israeli athletes. The Olympics was a battleground for political viewpoints throughout the decade. The nation of Taiwan was barred from the 1976 Olympics for wishing to call itself the Republic of China. South Africa withdrew from the Olympic movement to avoid a similar ban. New Zealand, a nation that continued international competition with South Africa, was permitted to participate in the 1976 Olympics—and twenty-nine other nations walked out in protest.

In less violent ways, the women's movement made its goals part of the sporting story of the decade. Women competed directly against men in some sports. Janet Guthrie became the first woman to compete in U.S. auto racing's premier event, the Indianapolis 500. Women jockeys became for the first time a familiar sight at major racetracks, with Robyn Smith becoming the first woman to ride a horse to victory in a stakes race at New York's Aqueduct track.

The decade's most highly publicized male vs. female event was the nationally televised tennis match in which Billie Jean King defeated Bobby Riggs. The National Little League allowed females to compete on formerly all-male teams. By the end of the decade, Ann Meyers had even signed a contract with a team in the formerly all-male National Basketball Association, though she did not play.

Above left: Billie Jean King was the most visible woman in sports, doing more than any other single person to ensure equality between women and men in sports. Above right: here signing autographs, Janet Guthrie became the first woman to drive in the Indianapolis 500. Opposite: Hank Aaron's 715th home run at Atlanta, April 8, 1974.

Legislation to ensure that women's sports would receive equal status with men's was part of Title IX of the Educational Amendments Act of 1972. It forbade educational institutions receiving federal aid from discriminating on the basis of sex. In the future, they would have to allot equal amounts of money for women's and men's sports programs, including athletic scholarship aid.

Professional women athletes began to demand, and receive, the higher monetary rewards formerly reserved for men. King, having collected $100,000 for her victory over Riggs, led women to demand prizes equal to men's at major tournaments such as Wimbledon and Forest Hills.

Throughout the world of sport, money occupied more headlines than scores or championships. In the three major professional sports, court decisions and player strikes paved the way for athletes to move more freely from team to team and command unbelievable salaries for their services. At the end of the 1976 season, baseball saw its first group of "free agents"—players who had played out the option year in their contracts and now had the right to sell their services to the highest bidder. Reggie Jackson became the highest paid of this group, signing with the New York Yankees for $2.9 million over five years. By the end of the decade that looked like a bargain, as Nolan Ryan signed with the Houston Astros for an estimated one million dollars a year, and several other players signed contracts at similarly high salaries. The highest payment for a single event, however, went to boxers Muhammad Ali and George Foreman, who each earned five million dollars for their bout in the African country of Zaire in 1974.

Ali was without doubt the biggest celebrity in sports. He dubbed himself "the Greatest," and his achievements led many to conclude that he was in fact the greatest boxer of all time.

Muhammad Ali was the best-known athlete in the world, both for his tremendous boxing skill and for his superstar personality.

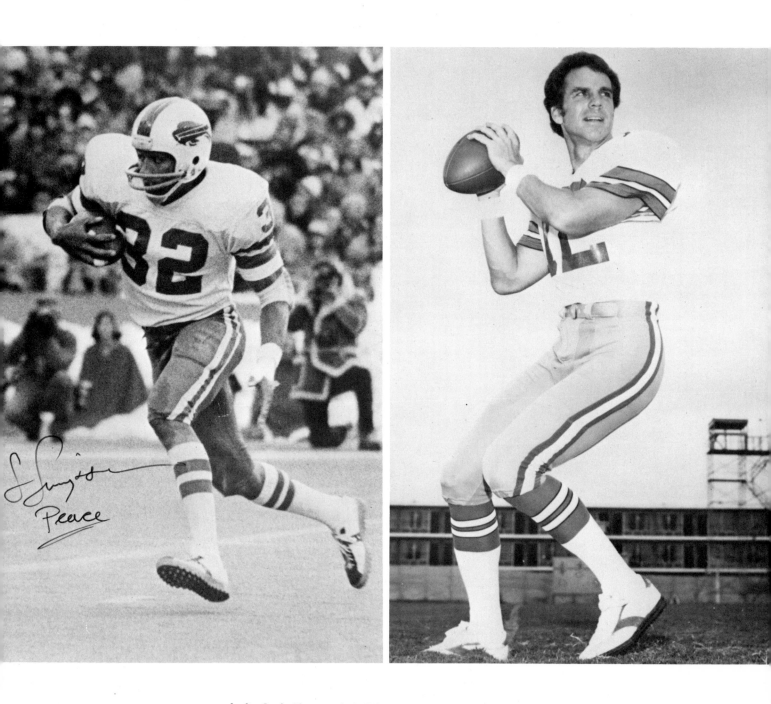

Left: O. J. Simpson's brilliant career with the Buffalo Bills and the San Francisco 49ers covered a decade. Right: Roger Staubach quarterbacked the Dallas Cowboys to victory in Super Bowl XII. Roger thrilled fans with his last-minute "bombs" that could turn a game around.

In baseball, three teams vied for the honor of team of the decade. The Oakland Athletics took three straight World Series from 1972 to 1974 with Reggie Jackson, Catfish Hunter, and Rollie Fingers among their leading players. Free agency and a tight-fisted owner dissolved the Oakland club. The "Big Red Machine" of Cincinnati, led by Pete Rose, Johnny Bench, Tony Perez, Joe Morgan, and George Foster, won the next two World Series. Cincinnati's 1975 victory over the Boston Red Sox was thought by some to be the greatest series ever played, highlighted by the sixth game, which Carlton Fisk won for Boston with a home run in the bottom of the twelfth inning. The New York Yankees won the series in 1977. The following season, after being fourteen games back of the Red Sox on July 19, the Yankees won the division title from the Red Sox in a one-game play-off, and went on to a second straight World Series victory. The Pittsburgh Pirates, calling themselves "the Family" after the words of a popular disco record, defeated Baltimore in the 1979 World Series after being down three games to one.

In professional football, the annual Super Bowl, which had begun in the previous decade as a demonstration of the National Football Conference's supremacy over the junior American Conference, soon assumed its importance as the most heavily viewed television sports event of the year. In 1973 the Miami Dolphins completed an unprecedented unbeaten season of fourteen regular-season games and three play-off games by defeating the Washington Redskins in Super Bowl VII. Miami repeated its Super Bowl win the following year, but, after the loss of key players to the short-lived World Football League, never regained the championship. The Pittsburgh Steelers, led by Terry Bradshaw, Franco Harris, and "Mean" Joe Greene, won the next two Super Bowls, and were followed by Oakland and Dallas in succeeding years. The Steelers regained their championship in Super Bowl XIII in January 1979.

Professional basketball was dominated by no single team, as players moved or were traded from team to team, preventing the growth of a dynasty. Basketball's lone consistent winner was at the college level, as UCLA, under Coach John Wooden, won eighty-eight straight games from 1971 to 1974, and collected NCAA championships in 1971, 1972, 1973, and 1975. Though Wooden never coached pro basketball, he provided that sport's only dynasty as two of his players—Kareem Abdul-Jabbar and Bill Walton—led their teams to

Opposite: Secretariat in 1973 became the first Triple Crown winner
in horse racing in twenty-five years. Brazilian soccer star Pelé
was famous throughout the world for his exploits in what most
nations called football. And Nadia Comaneci, the Rumanian gymnast,
was awarded perfect scores of 10 on the beam and the uneven bars—
the first perfect scores in gymnastics in Olympic history. Above:
Chris Evert's famous two-handed backhand was adopted by younger
players. She was acknowledged as the top woman tennis player
of the latter half of the decade. And Kareem Abdul-Jabbar was
the "biggest" star in any sport, standing 7′4″ tall, although
he himself claimed to be 7′2″. At his best, he was without question the greatest basketball player of this or any other decade.

three NBA titles. Walton won with the Portland Trail Blazers, and Abdul-Jabbar with two teams, the Milwaukee Bucks and the Los Angeles Lakers.

Golfing fans waited in vain for the one achievement that Jack Nicklaus never attained—the "Grand Slam," or victory in the four major golf tournaments in a single year. Though in 1973 Nicklaus won his fourteenth major title, more than any golfer before him, and added to the record throughout the decade, the closest he came to the fabled Slam was in 1975, when he won the Masters and PGA and missed the other two titles by a total of three strokes. In women's golf, Nancy Lopez made one of the most spectacular debuts of any first year player in any sport when in 1978 she won a record $161,235 while capturing nine tournament victories—five of them consecutively.

Billie Jean King's triumphs in tennis made her the premier woman in the sport in the early part of the decade. Teenager Chris Evert took her place at the top of the sport with four consecutive U.S. Open victories between 1975 and 1978. Evert was then dethroned by Tracy Austin who became the U.S. Open's youngest-ever champion in 1979 at the age of sixteen.

Evert's onetime fiancé, Jimmy Connors, was at or near the top of men's tennis for part of the decade, but Swedish star Bjorn Borg won four consecutive titles at Wimbledon, England, between 1976 and 1979 and was considered the top player in the world at the end of the decade.

Though the Olympics were a battleground for national and international politics, the sports events were individual affairs. In the 1972 Olympics, Russian gymnastics star Olga Korbut won two gold medals and a silver. The world fell in love with the 5' 1", 84 lb. teenager, and her achievements spurred increased interest in gymnastics in the United States. In the same Olympics, American swimmer Mark Spitz set world records in seven events, winning more gold medals than any other competitor in Olympic history.

In the Montreal Olympics of 1976, Rumania's Nadia Comaneci, then fourteen years old, took the spotlight. Surpassing Korbut's feats in gymnastics, she took three gold medals and a bronze. The United States's Bruce Jenner set a new world record in winning the decathlon. Though there was no standout swimming star of the caliber of Spitz, the United States men's teams won twelve of the thirteen swimming and diving events on an individual or team basis.

FACES IN THE CROWD

Miss Piggy was a real superstar even though she was only a Muppet. Jim Henson's Muppets were popular worldwide, as the stars of "Sesame Street," later of their own program "The Muppet Show," and finally of *The Muppet Movie.*

Right: Gary Gilmore was executed at the Utah state prison on January 17, 1977. It was the first execution in the United States since 1967. The case attracted worldwide publicity because of Gilmore's insistence that he be executed despite lawyers' attempts to gain a judicial reprieve. Capital punishment was a controversial subject throughout the decade. Below: Evel Knievel made himself famous, according to him, by breaking every bone in his body except his neck. He gained some notoriety for his stunts, which included jumping a motorcycle over everything from a series of parked cars to heaps of rattlesnakes. In the summer of 1974, the nation sought relief from Watergate by reading of his plans to jump Idaho's Snake River Canyon in a rocket-propelled vehicle. On September 8, he climbed into the "Sky-Cycle" for the attempt, but before he cleared the launch ramp, the vehicle's landing parachute was activated, sending it floating harmlessly to the bottom of the canyon.

Opposite: Patty Hearst, the wealthy heiress to the newspaper fortune, was kidnapped on February 5, 1974, touching off the decade's most bizarre crime story. Her kidnappers were the self-styled Symbionese Liberation Army, who released tape recordings announcing their demands that the Hearst family distribute food among poor families. In April 1974 the photograph shown here revealed that Patty had taken part in the SLA's robbery of a San Francisco bank. Despite a nationwide search, Ms. Hearst remained a fugitive for nineteen months. When she was finally apprehended on September 18, 1975, she gave her occupation as "urban guerrilla." A jury convicted her, and she spent time in jail.

Opposite: these two men conquered the World Trade Center (behind them), New York's tallest buildings. On the left is George Willig, who used equipment of his own design to climb up the side of the 110-story building. On the right is Philipe Petite, who crossed a tightrope between the two towers as office workers gaped from the street. Above: have you seen this man? Nobody has, since the night of November 24, 1971, when he parachuted from an airliner somewhere in the northwestern United States. Giving the name D. B. Cooper, he hijacked the airliner and collected a ransom of $200,000 before allowing the other passengers to disembark and forcing the crew to take off again.

Left: though ABC's Monday Night Football telecast showed a weekly NFL football game, its real stars were these three men: top, Howard Cosell (left) and Frank Gifford; below, "Dandy" Don Meredith. Cosell's acerbic comments and verbal hijinks, Meredith's wry wit, and Gifford's steady, knowledgeable play-by-play could make even the dullest game enjoyable.

Right: these were the original "Charlie's Angels" of the television program of the same name. At top is Farrah Fawcett-Majors. Below are Kate Jackson (left) and Jaclyn Smith. All three played former policewomen who now worked for a private detective, "Charlie," whose face was never seen. Fawcett-Majors was the pin-up star of the decade. Her billowy hair style prompted a national fad.

Howard Jarvis showed that one person can still have an influence on government. He sparked and led the 1978 "tax revolt" in California that successfully promoted the passage of Proposition 13, to limit property taxes. Afterward, Jarvis was in demand as a speaker on the tax structure of the state and national governments. Here he holds a news conference in front of the Internal Revenue Service building in Washington, D.C.

INDEX

Numbers in italics indicate photographs.